Echoes Of The Crone: Woven Through Time

21 Poems of Wisdom, Love, and Growth for the Maiden's Journey

Beth Aust

BookLeaf
Publishing

India | USA | UK

Made with ❤ on the BookLeaf Publishing Platform

www.bookleafpub.in

www.bookleafpub.com

Dedication

To my daughters, *Autumn, Mackenzie, and Holly*—this collection is for you. May these words serve as a reminder of the love and strength that runs through our family. Thank you for teaching me every day what it means to be a mother and a woman.

To all the *maidens on their journeys*, may you find the courage to walk your path with grace, wisdom, and the unwavering support of those who love you. And to those seeking a guiding light, may these poems illuminate your way.

To our *ancestral lineage*, whose wisdom and resilience have been passed down through the generations. Your strength is woven into the very fabric of who we are, and this is a humble tribute to you.

Preface

In the quiet corners of life, between the whirlwind of being a nurse, a wife, a mother, and now a crone, I've found my voice in the gentle art of poetry. This collection, *Woven in Time: Crone's Stories for the Maiden's Path*, is a reflection of the wisdom and love I've gathered over the years, woven together with the threads of my own journey. As a mother, I've had the privilege of watching my three beautiful daughters—and my sweet son—grow, finding their paths in this world. This is my offering to them, and to any maiden embarking on her own sacred journey. May these words inspire, comfort, and guide, just as the love of a mother can.

As I write alongside my youngest daughter, Holly, in a poetry challenge we share, I'm reminded of the preciousness of time. My own path has been marked by love, loss, and the ever-present desire to be the best version of myself for my children. Losing my own mother at 21 has been a shaping force in my life, and the greatest blessing is being here now, able to offer these words to my daughters and to any maiden who might find comfort and direction in them.

Acknowledgements

To my beloved daughters: Autumn, Mackenzie, and Holly. Your presence in my life is the greatest gift, and this collection is a reflection of the love and wisdom I've gathered from being your mother. I am blessed to be here for you, and you have been my greatest teachers. Thank you for inspiring me everyday.

To my son, whose kind heart fills our home with warmth and compassion. Your gentle spirit is a constant reminder of the beauty in the world, and I'm grateful to be your mom.

To my mother, who left this world too soon but remains in my heart forever. You are with me in every step I take, and in every word I write.

To my sisterhood, for their unwavering support and love through every chapter of my journey.
With humble gratitude to life itself, for the lessons it's brought, and for the blessing of being here for my children.

1. The Crone's Call

*Introduction to the wisdom of the crone and her
intention to guide younger women on their path.*

In the quiet of the twilight, she waits,
  A keeper of truths, a weaver of fates.
  Her hair, silvered threads of moonlight spun,
  Her wisdom a river where stories run.

"Come closer, my daughters, and hear my song",
  The echoes of women who've journeyed long.
  Each wrinkle, a map; each scar, a flame,
  Each choice, a stone in life's sacred game.

I offer no answers, no golden decree,
  But keys to unlock the crone you will be.
  Listen with your heart, not just with your ears,
  For truth often whispers through laughter and tears.

Together, we'll walk through the valleys of you,
  Through shadows, through light, through all you
construe.
  Take my hand, let the journey unfold—
  A story of wisdom, of courage, of gold.

2. Seeds of Self-Worth

Discovering and nurturing your inherent value.

Beneath the surface where doubt takes root,
 Lies soil rich with the truth's pursuit.
 A seed of worth, though hidden, resides,
 Waiting for sunlight, for water, for guides.

"*You are enough,*" the crone softly speaks,
 Not for what you do, but the soul that peaks.
 In the quiet moments when no one sees,
 You are the blossom, the wind, the trees.

No mirror can show what's carved in the stars,
 No word from another can heal those scars.
 It's you who must nurture, it's you who must tend,
 The garden within where self-love can mend.

Stand tall, my child, for your roots run deep,
 Through struggles, through triumphs, through all that
you keep.
 The seed is within, now give it its due—
 Water it daily, and it will bloom true

3. The Mirror of Self-Love

Exploring the power of accepting and loving yourself as you are.

The mirror gleams, a silent gaze,
Reflecting truths through shadowed haze.
Lines of doubt and tales untold,
Stories woven in scars of old.

"Look here," says the crone, her voice serene,
Not for perfection, but what lies between.
The curves, the edges, the tender, the raw—
This is your temple; revere it in awe.

No mirror is kind, nor always true,
Its glass holds nothing but a version of you.
Step closer, child, let your soul take the lead—
Love isn't found; it's a planted seed.

Trace the contours with forgiving hands,
Feel the strength where your spirit stands.
The mirror may glimmer, but it cannot see—
The love that blooms from inside thee

4. Gratitude's Golden Thread

How gratitude weaves joy and resilience into everyday life.

A golden thread through the tapestry flows,
Binding the heart to what it knows.
The morning's sun, the evening's rest,
Each moment a gift, each breath blessed.

"*Gratitude,*" whispers the crone with care,
Is not in the grand, but the everyday there.
In the song of the sparrow, the rustle of leaves,
In the warmth of the fire on winter's eves.

Do not wait for the mountain, the gilded prize,
For the joy of life lies in the simplest guise.
A hand held tightly, a laugh that rings,
A sky painted gold as the twilight sings.

Each thread you weave strengthens the soul,
Each thankful thought makes you whole.
Wrap yourself in this fabric divine—
Gratitude's golden thread will always shine

5. Laws of the Universe

Understanding universal truths and how they guide us—
like karma, attraction, and rhythm.

The stars above and the earth below,
Speak truths that only the wise will know.
Invisible laws, yet steady and strong,
Binding the cosmos, where we belong.

"*The law of cause, the law of effect,*"
The crone begins with quiet respect.
What you give, you'll gather; what you sow, you'll reap
—
Karma's lessons run timeless and deep.

Energy flows where your focus resides,
Shaping the world, the seas, and the tides.
Like attracts like, as thoughts create—
Your mind is the painter; your life is the slate.

Honor the rhythm, the ebb, and the flow,
There's a season for everything you'll ever know.
When you align with these truths profound,
You'll find your feet on sacred ground.

6. Dancing with Shadows

Facing challenges and dealing with difficult people with grace and strength.

The shadows rise, a daunting crowd,
Their voices sharp, their presence loud.
But within the dark, a lesson hides—
Growth is found where courage abides.

"*Not all will bring you kindness or care,*"
The crone observes with a knowing stare.
Some will challenge, some will deceive,
But even the thorns have truths to weave.

You cannot control the storms they bring,
But you can choose how your spirit will sing.
Hold your ground, let your light remain,
Their shadows can't dim what you sustain.

Dance with grace, but guard your flame,
Not every battle deserves your name.
Rise above, like the moon on high—
A beacon of strength in the darkest sky

7. Anchored in the Present

Practicing mindfulness to calm anxiety and find peace.

The mind, like a river, rushes and roars,
Carrying echoes, opening doors.
To the past, to the future, it leaps and it sways,
Rarely resting in the heart of today.

"Anchor yourself," the crone gently guides,
To the moment where stillness resides.
Feel the breath as it flows through your chest,
This is the home where your spirit finds rest.

The worry you carry, the fears that you keep,
Are clouds that drift but never seep.
Let them pass; let them fade—
Your peace is here, in the present laid.

Be with the wind, the earth, the sky,
Feel the weight of now, let the future lie.
Each moment is sacred, a gift to behold,
Be anchored, my child, let life unfold.

8. Rituals of Radiance

*Creating daily self-care habits that nourish the soul,
body, and mind.*

The sun greets the earth, the moon bids goodbye,
 In their rhythm, a lesson, their rituals apply.
 For life unfolds in steady streams,
 Shaped by habits, not by dreams.

"Feed your spirit, your body, your mind,"
 The crone advises, her voice aligned.
 Begin each day with an act of care—
 A sip of water, a breath of air.

Let each choice be a balm, each step a prayer,
 Tend to your temple with love and repair.
 Stretch your limbs, nourish your skin,
 Feed the fire that burns within.

At night, release what no longer serves,
 Honor your rest—it's what you deserve.
 Rituals of radiance will guide your way,
 Infusing light into every day.

9. Morning's Promise

Crafting a morning routine that sets the tone for an intentional day.

The dawn unfolds with gentle grace,
A quiet canvas, an open space.
Before the noise, before the race,
Morning offers its sacred embrace.

"*Rise with intention,*" the crone imparts,
For the day begins where the morning starts.
Sip the silence, let your soul ignite,
Set your compass by this soft light.

Stretch toward the sun, feel its gentle call,
Breathe in the promise that morning holds for all.
Whisper your gratitude, let it take flight,
Align your spirit before the fight.

The day may be heavy, the path unclear,
But morning's stillness will keep you near.
Each dawn is a promise, a chance anew—
To begin, to believe, to become more you.

10. The Sanctuary of Night

Evening rituals for reflection, release, and renewal.

As the sun slips low and the sky turns deep,
Night gathers all in her arms to keep.
The chaos quiets, the shadows grow,
A time to release, to let life flow.

"*Find your sanctuary,*" the crone softly says,
In the velvet hush of the day's endways.
Dim the lights, let the world recede,
Give your soul the rest it needs.

Write the burdens you've carried too long,
Fold them away with a soothing song.
Reflect on the gifts the day has brought,
Even the lessons, though hard they've taught.

Let the stars be your witness, the moon your guide,
To dreams where your spirit can safely reside.
For night is a sanctuary, a sacred rite,
To heal, to restore, and welcome the light.

11. Wealth of the Heart and Hand

Redefining financial abundance and building a meaningful relationship with money.

Gold can glitter, and riches may gleam,
But wealth is more than the surface dream.
It lives in the heart, in the love we give,
In the freedom to choose the life we live.

"Value your treasures," the crone declares,
But know that abundance begins in your cares.
Money's a tool, not the end you seek,
A servant of purpose, not power's peak.

Save with wisdom, spend with grace,
Let your choices reflect your truest place.
Wealth grows strong where intentions align—
A balance of giving, of yours and mine.

Do not chase shadows, nor hoard with fear,
For true abundance is always near.
It's found in enough, in a life well planned,
In the wealth of the heart and the work of your hand.

12. Threads of Spirit

Connecting with the divine, however it's defined—
through nature, meditation, or prayer.

The wind whispers secrets, the stars softly glow,
The threads of the spirit are woven below.
Invisible ties to the great unseen,
A force that hums through all that has been.

"Seek connection," the crone advises,
In the earth's embrace, where life arises.
Feel the breath of the trees, the pulse of the sea,
The divine lives in all; it lives in thee.

Through prayer, through stillness, or in the wild,
The spirit is found in the heart of a child.
In the quiet moments, the spaces between,
It calls to you softly, yet keenly serene.

Trust the threads that hold you tight,
A tapestry woven of love and light.
When you feel untethered, lost in the fray,
The spirit will guide you back to your way.

13. The Body's Temple

Honoring physical well-being through care, movement, and nourishment.

Your body, a temple, sacred and rare,
A vessel of strength, deserving of care.
It carries your spirit, your heart, your fire,
Treat it with love, with mindful desire.

"Feed it well," the crone implores,
With foods that heal, that open doors.
Move it gently, let it sing,
For motion is life; it's everything.

Rest when it's weary, listen with grace,
Each ache and whisper holds its place.
Your body's a partner, not just a tool—
To ignore its wisdom is the gravest fool.

Treat it as holy, this gift you've been given,
A bridge between earth and the heavens you're living.
When you honor this temple, inside and out,
You'll feel its strength, beyond any doubt.

14. Love's Infinite Faces

Understanding love in its many forms—romantic, platonic, and selfless.

Love wears many faces, both fierce and soft,
A tempest below, a calm aloft.
It's found in a friend, in a lover's embrace,
In the quiet moments time can't erase.

"Love is not bound," the crone gently sighs,
By who or how, by limits or ties.
It's found in the giving, in the shared light,
In holding another through their darkest night.

But start with yourself; it begins there,
A heart filled with love is a heart that can share.
Don't chase it, don't force it—let love arrive,
In its own wild way, it keeps us alive.

It's the bond that heals, the thread that connects,
The power to soften life's sharpest effects.
Love's infinite faces, so varied, so true,
Are all reflections of the divine in you.

15. The Fight for Justice

*Embracing human rights and standing against injustice
with courage and compassion.*

The world can be cruel, its balance askew,
But justice is born in hearts that are true.
A voice may be small, but it carries might,
When it rises for others, for what is right.

"Stand tall," says the crone, her eyes alight,
Speak for the silenced, fight the good fight.
For freedom and dignity, for lives oppressed,
Your courage will honor the world's distressed.

Know that justice is not always swift,
It demands your patience, your strength, your gift.
But each step forward, no matter how small,
Builds a foundation for justice to call.

Wear your empathy like a shield,
Let your compassion be the sword you wield.
In the fight for justice, together we'll strive,
To create a world where all can thrive.

16. Embracing the Wholeness of Life

Finding harmony by integrating all aspects of life into a balanced whole.

Life is a puzzle, with pieces wide,
Joy and sorrow walk side by side.
The light and the shadow, the ebb and the flow,
Together they shape the life we know.

"*Do not fear the contrasts,*" the crone advises,
For in their union, the soul arises.
The laughter, the tears, the struggle, the peace—
Each moment is part of your soul's release.

Balance is found in the dance, not the still,
In learning to bend with life's shifting will.
Honor the seasons, the highs and the lows,
Each is a teacher, each helps you grow.

To live is to weave all threads into one,
Under the moon, beneath the sun.
Embrace the wholeness, the depth, the strife,
For this is the fullness of a human life.

17. The Power of Patience

*Learning the value of patience and trusting the process
of growth and change.*

The seed is planted, the earth is still,
 A quiet promise beneath the hill.
 Though nothing stirs, it's not in vain—
 The roots are growing, though unseen by the plain.

"Patience, my dear," the crone imparts,
 Is the silent force that guides the heart.
 You cannot rush what's meant to grow,
 Nor speed the winds that must blow slow.

Trust in time, though it may seem long,
 For seasons will pass and you'll be strong.
 Each moment a step in your journey's grace,
 A path unfolding at its own pace.

The oak doesn't rush to reach the sky,
 Nor the river to carve its way, passing by.
 Patience is knowing, in your bones, in your soul,
 That all will come when the time makes you whole.

18. The Dance of the Divine Feminine

Honoring the sacred feminine energy that exists within all, regardless of gender.

She flows like a river, fierce and free,
A force of nature, a deep, wild sea.
The divine feminine, ancient and wise,
Exists within us all, beneath every disguise.

"She is the earth," the crone explains,
She is the moon, she is the rain.
She is the wildness, the softness, the fire—
The essence of life, the heart's desire.

Honor her rhythm, the cycles she brings,
The birth, the death, the spread of wings.
For the feminine is not just one thing—
She's every woman, every dream, every spring.

You, too, carry this sacred power,
A wellspring of strength in every hour.
Embrace the dance, let it be your guide—
For the divine feminine lives inside.

19. The Alchemy of Forgiveness

The transformative power of letting go of grudges and healing through forgiveness.

Forgiveness is not a gift for them,
But a balm for the heart, a gentle gem.
It is not weakness, nor a silent plea,
But a freedom that sets your spirit free.

"The burden of anger," the crone declares,
Is a weight too heavy, too much to bear.
Let go of the chains that bind your soul,
Forgiveness will make you fully whole.

It doesn't mean you forget or condone,
It means you release, and let it be known,
That peace comes when you clear the air,
When you no longer hold the past in despair.

Forgiveness is alchemy, turning pain into light,
A sacred magic that brings peace to the night.
Let it flow through you, gentle and true,
And watch as your heart begins to renew.

20. The Art of Letting Go

Releasing attachments and embracing the flow of life with open hands.

The river flows without holding tight,
The leaves drift down from branches light.
The sky offers clouds that come and go,
A lesson in release we all must know.

"Let go, dear one," the crone whispers low,
For life's true gift is in the ebb and the flow.
To hold too tightly is to strangle the air,
To release is to trust, to know you're cared.

Let go of what no longer serves,
Of plans that crumble, of dreams that swerve.
Release the need for control, for grasp,
And feel the freedom in each open clasp.

In letting go, we find what's true,
A space for new life, for something new.
So release the weight, the need to hold,
And watch your life unfold like gold.

21. The Legacy of Wisdom

Passing on the lessons learned and leaving a lasting impact on the world.

Time is a river, always flowing,
  Carrying wisdom, always growing.
  The years may pass, the seasons turn,
  But the lessons we learn, forever burn.

"You, my child," the crone's voice softens,
  Are the keeper of wisdom, the light that brightens.
  What you've learned, what you've seen,
  Is a treasure to pass to those yet to glean.

Legacy isn't wealth, nor fame to seek,
  It's in the love we share, the truths we speak.
  It's in the hearts we touch, the lives we change,
  In every small act, in every exchange.

So share your story, pass on the flame,
  For the world is richer for the lessons we claim.
  The legacy of wisdom, a path so wide,
  Guides future hearts with love as its guide.

www.ingramcontent.com/pod-product-compliance
Lightning Source LLC
LaVergne TN
LVHW010259210726
843508LV00020B/2894